Animal Neighbours

Badger

Michael Leach

Wayland

An imprint of Hodder Children's Books

Animal Neighbours

Titles in this series:

Badger • Deer • Fox • Hare • Hedgehog • Otter

Conceived and produced for Hodder Wayland by

Nutshell
MEDIA

Intergen House, 65–67 Western Road, Hove BN3 2JQ, UK
www.nutshellmedialtd.co.uk

Commissioning Editor: Victoria Brooker
Editor: Polly Goodman
Designer: Tim Mayer
Illustrator: Jackie Harland

Published in Great Britain in 2003 by Hodder Wayland, an imprint of Hodder Children's Books.

British Library Cataloguing in Publication Data
Leach, Michael, 1954–
Badger. – (Animal neighbours)
1. Badgers – Juvenile literature
I.Title
599.7'672

ISBN 0 7502 4166 7

Printed and bound in Hong Kong

Hodder Children's Books
A division of Hodder Headline Limited
338 Euston Road, London NW1 3BH

Cover photograph: A badger foraging for food at night in a woodland.
Title page: A badger raids a dustbin looking for scraps of food. Badgers are becoming a more familiar sight in many towns and cities.

Picture acknowledgements
FLPA 6 (Gerard Laci), 8, 10 (Martin B. Withers), 12 (John Tinning), 13 (E. & D. Hosking), 19 (Martin B. Withers), 27 (John Tinning), 28 top & bottom left (Martin B. Withers); Michael Leach 20, 21; NHPA *Cover* (Andy Rouse), 7 (Manfred Danegger), 17, 24 (Andy Rouse), 25 (Manfred Danegger), 26 (Laurie Campbell); Oxford Scientific Films *Title page* (Robin Redfern), 9 (Bill Paton), 11, 14 (Robin Redfern), 16 (Mark Hamblin), 22, 23, 28 right & top right (Robin Redfern).

Contents

Meet the Badger

The badger is a powerful member of the weasel family. There are nine species of badger alive today. They live mostly in woodlands and can be found throughout the world, except in Australia and South America.

This book looks at the Eurasian badger – the most widespread species in the world.

▲ The red shading on this map shows where badgers live in the world today.

Fur

Badgers have thick fur to protect them from the cold.

Body

Badgers have low, powerful bodies that are perfectly shaped for tunnelling through soil.

Scent gland

Near the base of the tail is a scent gland, which is used to mark the badger's territory with a strong smell.

The Eurasian badger. ▶

Claws

The badger has powerful feet with long, curved claws. These are ideal tools for digging, when looking for food or making a sett.

◀ **The badger is larger than a domestic cat.**

BADGER FACTS

The Eurasian badger's scientific name is *Meles meles*. This comes from the Latin word *meles*, meaning 'badger'.

Males are known as boars, females as sows and young badgers as cubs.

Adult boars measure about 75 cm long and weigh up to 15 kg. Sows are slightly smaller. They are 72 cm long and weigh up to 13 kg.

Ears

Badgers have an excellent sense of hearing, which they use to detect danger. When they hear something unfamiliar they often run or disappear into their dens.

Eyes

Badgers have poor eyesight and cannot see well over long distances.

Snout

The badger's snout is used to push through soft earth and undergrowth while looking for food.

Nose

Badgers have an excellent sense of smell. They keep their sensitive noses close to the ground to help follow the scent of other badgers, detect enemy tracks and find suitable food.

Teeth

Badgers have long, sharp canine teeth towards the front, which are used for self-defence and killing prey. Behind the canines are large, flat teeth for chewing.

Whiskers

The badger's long whiskers act as 'feelers', allowing it to move around dark underground tunnels by touch.

5

The Weasel Family

The badger is one of 67 species belonging to the weasel family. Other members of the family include otters, weasels, skunks and mink. All animals in this family have long bodies and short legs. They are all predators, hunters of other animals, but they are shy animals that are difficult to find.

Badgers all around the world are a similar size and shape, but each species has its own unique behaviour, specially suited to its habitat. The Oriental ferret badgers of Asia usually live in tropical rainforests. They are one of the few species of badger that climb trees, feeding on insects and fruit found high above the ground.

▼ Sea otters spend all their lives in the water. They float on their backs when eating (like this one) and sleeping.

The honey badger of Africa makes its home in sandy deserts and even on mountainsides. American badgers are very different to their cousins in Europe. They live alone and prefer to come out in daylight, unless humans are nearby.

BIGGEST AND SMALLEST

The biggest member of the weasel family is the sea otter, which lives in the Pacific Ocean off the west coast of North America. It measures up to 1.6 m long and can weigh up to 45 kg. The smallest member is the least weasel, which is only 20 cm long and weighs just 70 g.

Pine martens are members of the ▶ weasel family. They are skilful climbers that hunt birds and mammals both on the ground and high in the tree tops.

Birth and Growing Up

Badger cubs are born in the spring, in an underground den called a sett. The sett is a maze of connected tunnels containing many underground chambers (see pages 14–15).

New-born badger cubs are blind and deaf, born with their eyes and ears tightly closed. But their sense of smell is already very good. Inside the dark sett, they learn to identify their mother by her scent. Only at about 3 weeks old do their eyes open. They can crawl from birth, but do not begin to walk properly until their eyes are fully open.

▲ These 4-week-old cubs huddle together to keep warm while their mother is out hunting.

BADGER CUBS

New-born badger cubs are about 12 cm long with a 3-cm-long tail. They weigh about 100 g.

The cubs are born covered with short grey fur. Black face stripes only begin to appear about a week after birth.

A sow normally gives birth to a litter of three badger cubs, although it can be between one and four. She produces just one litter a year.

▲ A 9-month-old cub (left) with its mother in the sett. Badger cubs like to stay with their mother for as long as possible, but as they grow bigger, the sett becomes very overcrowded.

During the day the sow leaves her cubs and sleeps in another chamber in the same sett. When the sun goes down, she leaves the sett to find food, but comes back several times during the night to suckle her cubs.

Leaving the sett

The badger cubs first leave the sett at about 8 weeks old, but they stay close to the entrance at all times. If danger threatens, they run underground immediately. In these early weeks, the cubs spend hours digging holes, chasing each other and playing with sticks.

At about 12 weeks old, the cubs eat their first solid food. Their mother carries the food back to them in her stomach. With a few short coughs, she pushes the food up and out through her mouth. The cubs swallow it hungrily, fighting to get their share. For the next few months, the cubs take food from their mother and still suckle her milk. By the age of 16 weeks they are weaned and eat the same food as adult badgers.

▼ These 14-week-old cubs often play-fight. This strengthens their muscles and is good practice for the time when they need to hunt and defend themselves.

▲ Four cubs carefully sniff the air for danger before leaving the safety of the sett.

Throughout the summer the young cubs follow their mother every night, learning what to eat and where to find it. In the autumn they become independent and start to feed alone. Some cubs leave the home sett immediately and join another group of badgers, while others stay until the following year and then leave. The rest stay permanently in the sett where they were born.

BADGER CALLS

Badgers use many different sounds to communicate:

- A deep, low growl is a threat signal, telling enemies or other badgers to keep away.

- A short bark is a sign that the badger is surprised.

- A long, penetrating scream is used when the badger is very frightened.

- Short, sharp chattering calls show a badger is excited. Cubs produce these sounds when they are playing.

11

Habitat

▲ Woodlands contain a huge variety of insects, but badgers have to work hard to find them.

The badger's favourite habitat is woodland, but since many woodlands have been destroyed over the last 100 years, badgers have had to learn to live in other habitats. Badger setts can now be found under hedgerows, on moorland and open farmland. As towns and cities have grown, some setts have become surrounded by new houses. These urban badgers have learned to make their homes in parks, gardens and even under buildings.

Badgers prefer to build their setts in thick undergrowth. This lets them enter and leave unnoticed and provides a safe place for their young cubs to play. Although badgers can swim very well, they do not build their setts in wet areas because of the risk of them being flooded.

Some people believe that badgers hibernate in winter, but this is not true. They simply become less active to save energy when there is not much food around. On cold, wet nights they often do not come out of the sett at all. The underground dens are warm and dry, and the badgers have enough body fat to allow them to last several days without eating.

▼ Badgers have only recently learned to raid rubbish bags and bins looking for food scraps thrown away by humans.

WARNING MARKS

Most nocturnal animals are camouflaged to hide them from their enemies, but badgers do not have many enemies. Their strength and powerful bite mean that they could kill most other animals that share their habitat. So instead of camouflage, a badger's striped face is easily seen, even at night. The stripes warn other animals to keep away.

The sett

Inside each badger sett there are different chambers. Some chambers are for sleeping. These are just big enough for two badgers to lie next to each other. Breeding chambers are larger, with space for an adult sow and up to four cubs. Badgers dig new tunnels and chambers every year, so the size and design of the sett is always changing. As new entrances appear, others are abandoned.

In large territories, badgers occasionally have extra dens away from the main sett. These are just one or two holes on the edge of the territory. They are sometimes used for a few days during the summer, before the badgers return to the main sett.

▲ A badger at the entrance to its sett.

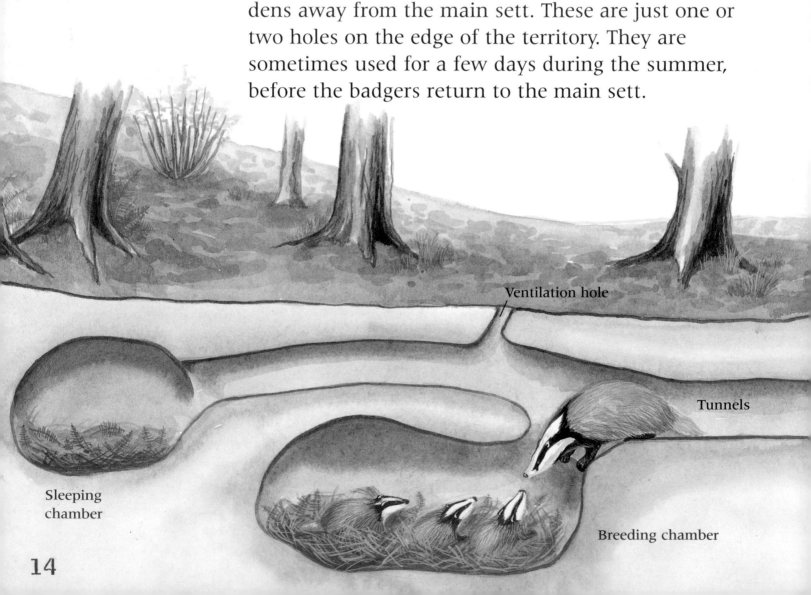

Ventilation hole

Tunnels

Sleeping chamber

Breeding chamber

Mice, voles and rabbits have all been found living in badger setts, even though badgers like to eat these animals. Foxes occasionally share the sett, but badgers do not like their strong smell and often drive them out. Old badger setts are often used as breeding dens by wild cats, pine martens and even wolves.

DIGGING THE SETT

Each sett can have 20 entrances, each about 25 cm in diameter. The entrances lead to tunnels that can be 100 m long.

Badgers dig using their front paws and push the loose soil out with their back legs. A badger can dig a deep tunnel in less than 2 minutes.

Badgers close their ears when they are digging by pushing the back of each ear forward to touch the front. This stops soil and stones falling in their ears and blocking their hearing.

▼ All badger setts are different. Only a few holes can be seen from the outside, but beneath the ground is a maze of connected tunnels and chambers.

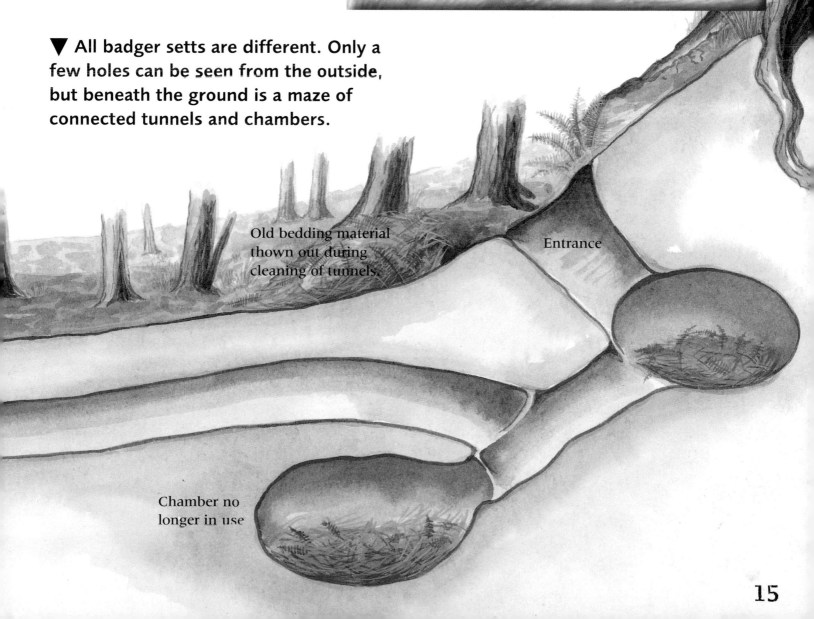

Old bedding material thown out during cleaning of tunnels.

Entrance

Chamber no longer in use

Territory

Eurasian badgers live in groups of up to 12, all sharing the same sett. Each group has its own territory of up to 15 square kilometres. They regularly mark the boundaries of the territory with heaps of fresh droppings. They also rub against rocks and trees, covering them with a strong-smelling liquid produced by their scent glands. These scent signals warn badgers from other groups to keep away.

Badgers from neighbouring setts usually obey the scent signals, but when food is scarce, they will leave their own territory in search of new feeding grounds. If they wander into the territory of another group, they are often attacked by males of the group.

▼ This badger is cleaning its claws on a tree trunk, which acts as a scratching post close to the sett.

Fights are most common in the spring, when badgers are being careful to defend their young cubs. These battles can be violent and involve several badgers. As the animals push and bite each other using their sharp teeth and long claws, the injuries are often serious and sometimes end in death. Old badgers often bear the scars of fights.

Badgers normally eat ▶ alone, but when there is plenty of food available they sometimes feed together. This large group is taking food left out for them on a garden patio.

BULLDOZERS

Badgers' heads are protected by a thick layer of jaw muscles that wrap around the side of the head and anchor on to a special bone on top of the skull. This protective layer means badgers can survive light blows to the head without serious injury. In fights, they use their heads like bulldozers, pushing and shoving their opponent in a test of strength.

Food

Badgers are omnivores, which means they will eat almost anything. Their exact diet changes throughout the year, depending on the food available. For much of the year they eat mainly earthworms, but they also eat a wide variety of other prey, including slugs, frogs, birds' eggs and a huge variety of insects.

▼ **Badgers have no natural enemies, so they are at the top of their food chain. (The illustrations are not to scale).**

Badger food chain

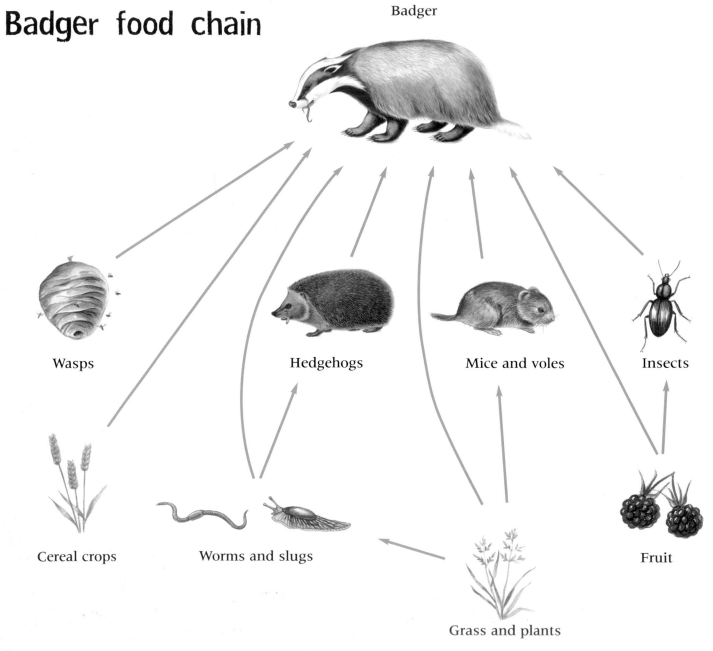

Badger

Wasps

Hedgehogs

Mice and voles

Insects

Cereal crops

Worms and slugs

Fruit

Grass and plants

In the summer, badgers eat ripe cereal crops for a short time. Autumn brings a rich harvest of fruit and nuts, which provides plenty of food. Badgers particularly like eating apples, acorns, hazelnuts, raspberries and blackberries. They eat grass and clover throughout the year.

▼ Badgers often use their powerful jaws to rip open rotten logs and eat the insects hiding inside.

WORMS

In the summer, a badger can eat 700 worms in a single night. During winter, when the ground is frozen hard and the worms stay deep down in the soil, a badger may go without a single worm for several weeks.

Finding meat

Badgers like eating meat, but they cannot run fast enough to catch big animals. They occasionally eat carrion, often the bodies of animals killed by road traffic. They find mice and voles using their excellent sense of smell to seek out breeding dens hidden deep in undergrowth. The adult mice usually escape, but the young are easily caught and eaten.

Badgers are one of the few animals that are strong enough to eat hedgehogs. They use their powerful claws to unroll a curled-up hedgehog, avoiding being injured by the sharp spines. In towns and cities, badgers have learned to look for new types of food. Many badgers now raid dustbins, searching for scraps of fat and meat to eat.

Badgers always search for food and eat alone. Only sows with young cubs stay close together during feeding. Every sunset, badgers leave the sett, spending a few minutes scratching and stretching before wandering away separately to look for food. Each animal spends up to ten hours a night digging through soil, carefully picking up worms with its lips.

▼ Badgers will eat almost any food from human rubbish. Meat and sweet foods are favourites.

BEACH BADGERS

Badgers are excellent at adapting to whatever food can be found close to the sett. Badgers living on the coast often eat mussels found on the beach. Their powerful jaws have no difficulty cracking open the hard shell to reach the soft mussel hidden inside.

Finding a Mate

After the age of one year, sows are ready to breed. Boars are not usually ready until they reach the age of two, when they are strong enough to fight off other males. Boars know when a sow is ready to mate because she produces a special scent. Badgers will mate many times with several partners, usually from their own sett.

Although most mating takes place in the spring and early summer, it can happen at any time of the year. Badgers are unusual mammals because the eggs do not grow inside the female immediately after mating. They may not begin to develop for

◄ Sows do most of the digging of the sett.

nearly nine months. This guarantees that all cubs are born in the spring, when there is plenty of food around.

The cubs are born about seven weeks after the eggs start growing. As the pregnant sow gets ready to give birth, she digs out a new chamber close to one of the sett's entrance holes.

▼ Badgers are very clean animals. They do not like wet or smelly bedding. Old grass is dragged out of the sett and replaced by fresh new undergrowth.

WHAT'S THE DIFFERENCE?

Male and female badgers look very similar, but there are differences. Boars are slightly heavier and bigger than sows, and they have a wider head. Sows have hairier tails. A badger can immediately tell the sex of another badger by its scent.

Threats

Fully grown badgers are so strong that they have no natural enemies, and many die simply of old age. Badgers can live for about 15 years in the wild. However, cubs are sometimes killed by large predators such as wolves, lynx and eagle owls. Young badgers need to keep close to their mother at all times because she will attack any enemy that gets too close.

For centuries, humans killed badgers for their fur. The thick skins made very warm clothes and the long, fine hairs were made into shaving brushes and artists' paint brushes. Badgers are now protected in many countries and are no longer hunted.

▼ Badger cubs have short, soft fur that was once used to make clothes. Many young badgers were killed every year until the tradition died out.

Some landowners do not like badgers because they can damage crops. Badgers will eat cereals such as oats and wheat, and they occasionally knock down growing plants while looking for food. Some farmers worry that cattle will fall into badger setts and injure themselves. Badger killing is illegal in most countries but every year, many are shot and gassed by farmers who want to drive the animals off their land.

▼ European eagle owls are among the few predators large enough to kill a badger cub.

Road traffic

Today the badger's greatest enemy is road traffic. Badgers are creatures of habit and use the same paths throughout their lives. Some paths are more than a century old and were first used long before cars and lorries were invented. Many of these ancient routes have now become very dangerous – for both people and badgers. When drivers swerve to avoid a badger on the road, they can cause an accident. Cars can be badly damaged if they hit a fully grown badger.

▲ Signs like this one are sometimes used to warn motorists that badgers may be crossing the road ahead.

Every year many badgers die as they cross roads to reach feeding sites. In some places conservationists have built special tunnels under roads, so that the badgers can still find food but avoid the traffic.

BADGER BAITING

Badgers were once caught and made to fight with dogs for public entertainment. Each badger would be put into a pit with three or four dogs. This was called badger baiting and took place in towns and cities around Europe. Baiting is now against the law, but it still goes on in a few remote places.

▼ Badger tunnels like this one beneath roads are now also used by other animals such as otters and deer.

Badger Life Cycle

1 The new-born badger cub is blind and weighs just 100 g. It is one of a litter of one to four cubs.

2 Three weeks after birth, the badger's eyes open for the first time.

6 Sows first breed when they are a year old. Boars are usually 2 years old before they mate.

3 At 8 weeks old, the cubs leave the sett for the first time.

5 At 8 months old, the badger cubs become independent and find their own food.

4 At the age of 12 weeks, badger cubs eat their first solid food.

Badger Clues

Look out for the following clues to help you find signs of a badger:

Setts
A series of holes in the ground, 20–50 cm in diameter. Setts are usually found in a wood, but occasionally in hedgerows or even in open fields. They smell slightly sweet if you walk past.

Soil heaps
Badger setts are surrounded by huge heaps of soil, created when the animals dig new chambers and tunnels. The soil usually contains dried grass, which is old bedding that has been replaced and thrown out. Look in the soil for long, black and white hairs amongst the grass.

Hair
Tufts of black and white fur caught on a fence show that a badger has pushed itself under during the night.

Droppings
Badgers leave their droppings in shallow pits close to the sett.

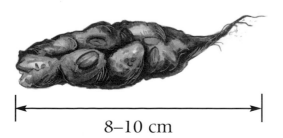

8–10 cm

Trails
Badgers use the same paths every night as they travel from the sett to good feeding grounds. They leave worn paths in the grass and make low tunnels through hedgerows.

Skulls and bones
When badgers die underground, their bodies are covered over by other badgers in the same sett. In later years, the skeletons can be dug up and the bones found scattered by the sett entrance.

Footprints
The footprints of badgers are about 4.5 cm long and clearly show a wide pad with five toes.

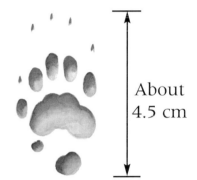

About 4.5 cm

Scratches on trees
Most setts have a tree nearby with scratch marks on the bark up to about 1 m high. These are probably used by badgers to clean their claws.

Diggings
Badgers dig shallow scrapes in the grass when they look for worms.

Glossary

boar A male badger.

camouflage The colour or pattern of some animals that helps them blend in with their surroundings and makes them hard to see.

canine teeth Long, sharp teeth towards the front of the mouth, used for killing and tearing meat.

carrion The body of a dead animal that is found and eaten by another animal.

cereal crops Crops such as wheat, barley and maize, which produce grain that is used for food.

conservationists People who want to protect wildlife and nature from harm.

habitat The area where an animal or plant naturally lives.

hibernate To sleep deeply through the whole winter.

litter A group of young animals born at the same time from the same mother.

nocturnal An animal that sleeps during the day and is active at night.

omnivore An animal that eats both meat and plants.

predator An animal that kills and eats other animals.

prey An animal that is killed and eaten by other animals.

sett The underground den of the badger.

sow A female badger.

suckle When a mother allows her young to drink milk from her teats.

territory An area that an animal or group of animals defend against others of the same species.

tracks The footprints and other signs left by an animal as it walks or runs.

tropical To do with the tropics, the regions north and south of the Equator.

urban A habitat in a town or city.

weaned A young mammal is weaned when it stops taking milk from its mother and eats only solid food.

Finding Out More

Other books to read

Animal Young: Mammals by Rod Theodorou (Heinemann, 1999)

Animal Neighbours: Otter by Michael Leach (Hodder Wayland, 2003)

Animal Sanctuary by John Bryant (Open Gate Press, 1999)

Badger by Michael Clark (Whittet, 1988)

Badgers by John Darbyshire & Laurie Campbell (Colin Baxter Photography, 1997)

Classification: Animal Kingdom by Kate Whyman (Hodder Wayland, 2000)

Collins Nature Guides: Garden Wildlife of Britain and Europe by Michael Chinery (Collins Natural History, 1997)

The Giant Book of Creatures of the Night by *Jim Pipe* (Watts, 1998)

Life Cycles: Cats and Other Mammals by Sally Morgan (Belitha, 2001)

Living with Urban Wildlife by John Bryant (Open Gate Press, 2002)

New Encyclopedia of Mammals by David Macdonald (OUP, 2001)

A True Book: Badgers by Joan Kalbacken (Children's Press, 1997)

The Wayland Book of Common British Mammals by Shirley Thompson (Hodder Wayland, 2000)

What's the Difference?: Mammals by Stephen Savage (Hodder Wayland, 1998)

Wild Britain: Woodlands; Parks & Gardens; Meadows by R. & L. Spilsbury (Heinemann, 2001)

Zoobooks: Skunks and their Relatives by Timothy L. Biel (Wildlife Education, 2001)

Organisations to contact

Countryside Foundation for Education
PO Box 8
Hebden Bridge HX7 5YJ
www.countrysidefoundation.org.uk
Training and teaching materials
to help people understand the
countryside and its problems.

The Mammal Society
15 Cloisters House
8 Battersea Park Road
London SW8 4BG
www.mammal.org.uk
Promotes the study and conservation
of British mammals.

Wildlife Watch
National Office
The Kiln
Waterside
Mather Road
Newark NG24 1WT
www.wwt.org.uk
The junior branch of the Wildlife Trusts, a
network of local Wildlife Trusts caring for
nearly 2,500 nature reserves, from rugged
coastline to urban wildlife havens, protecting
a huge number of habitats and species.

Index

Page numbers in **bold** refer to a photograph or illustration.